TREASURED

A 30-Day Devotional Journey

By Deb Burma

You are the Lord's treasured possession!

Deb Burma

CONCORDIA PUBLISHING HOUSE · SAINT LOUIS

Begin your daily devotion time in prayer

Heavenly Father,
Thank You for choosing me to be Your treasured
possession! I praise You for the gifts of forgiveness and
eternal life in Christ, as You have proclaimed them to me
in Your Word! As I read this devotion, fill me with Your
Holy Spirit, that I may continue to be transformed, grow-
ing in faith as I treasure Your Word and receive strength
for each new day. In Jesus' precious name. Amen.

Copyright © 2010 Concordia Publishing House
3558 S. Jefferson Avenue, St. Louis, MO 63118
1-800-325-3040 • www.cph.org

Manufactured in the United States of America

1 2 3 4 5 6 7 8 9 10   19 18 17 16 15 14 13 12 11 10

INTRODUCTION

What could be more precious than diamonds? YOU!

"The LORD has chosen you to be a people for His treasured possession" (Deuteronomy 14:2). You are the precious, priceless possession of your heavenly Father, who sought you and claimed you as His own in Christ. You are tenderly treasured by the Lord, who paid the ultimate price for you when He sent His Son to die in your place, filling you with the riches of His forgiveness and grace, and giving you the greatest treasure of all, the promise of eternal life in Him. From a plain old lump of coal to a dazzling diamond, you are continually being transformed in Christ. You shine brilliantly, by the power of the Holy Spirit, and you reflect His glory and light into a dark world in need of a Savior.

Just as a treasure hunter searches for hidden jewels and buried riches, you can seek out and treasure God's Word. Set aside some time each day to open the Bible and take a look at His treasures for you. The value of His Word is far greater than the value of any earthly treasure. God's precious Word points the way to Christ, "in whom are hidden all the treasures of wisdom and knowledge" (Colossians 2:3).

I pray that God would use these devotions to touch your heart with hope and joy in Christ, strengthen you in your daily walk with Him, and remind you that you are a treasured child of God, chosen to carry the priceless treasure of the Gospel to the world!

Serving Christ,

Deb Burma, author

A Chosen and Valuable Treasure

The LORD has chosen you to be a people for His
treasured possession. Deuteronomy 14:2

A dirty, dark lump of coal at the bottom of a coal mine. That is what you were when God chose you. You were not only stained in sin and surrounded by darkness, but that darkness made you like coal in the depths of a mine because you were conceived and born in sin. When God staked His claim on you, He excavated you from the pit and rescued you, bringing you up to the light. He lifted you out of the depths of the darkness of your sin, holding you in the palm of His hand, choosing you as His valuable, treasured possession. How could a chosen lump of coal have any value at all? Dr. Reed Lessing, professor at Concordia Seminary, shared in a message at a National Youth Gathering, "You were not chosen because you were valuable; you are valuable because you were chosen."

The world would see a plain old lump of coal as dirty, inside and out, and worthless if not for its use as a fuel source or even the punishment in a naughty child's Christmas stocking. But God saw the potential of your sparkle even then! God chose you just as you were. "God shows His love for us in that while we were still sinners, Christ died for us" (Romans 5:8). He didn't wait for you to try to clean yourself up or get your act together. He chose you and saved you from your sin when He washed you clean, inside and out, through the miraculous work of His Holy Spirit in your Baptism or when you heard God's Word proclaimed and the Holy Spirit first worked faith in your heart through the Word.

Yes, God loved you and chose you just as you were. But He didn't want you to remain that way, a simple piece of coal. He strengthens you "with power through His Spirit in your inner being, so that Christ may dwell in your hearts through faith . . . that you may be filled with all the fullness of God" (Ephesians 3:16–17, 19). Through the power of the Holy Spirit, Christ lives in you and grows in you. The Spirit continues its strengthening work, through God's amazing transformation process, changing you to have a heart like Christ's.

You are "filled with all the fullness of God" so you may reflect His image in Christ to a world in need of a Savior. While coal is not capable of reflection, the substance toward which the dirty lump of coal is headed, through its amazing transformation process, *does* reflect beautifully. Do you know what you are becoming? Do you know what precious gem is formed from coal? It's not gold or silver, but "a girl's best friend." The most precious of all minerals, the costliest of all gems: a diamond! As God's dearly-loved daughter, a hand-selected lump of coal, you are a valuable treasure, a DIAMOND in the making!

> *Lord, thank You for choosing me as Your treasured*
> *possession. Let Your Holy Spirit work in my heart, that*
> *I would be continually strengthened and transformed,*
> *becoming more like Christ, reflecting His image*
> *to the world. In His name I pray. Amen.*

A Diamond in the Making,
Part 1: Time

He who began a good work in you will bring it to
completion at the day of Jesus Christ.
Philippians 1:6

Once upon a time, you were just a plain old, dirty lump of coal; and yet you were chosen in the depths of the darkness of your sin to be God's treasured possession in Christ! He hand-selected you and purchased you to be His own dear daughter. He bought you with His Son's blood; Jesus' death and resurrection paid for you, saving you from your sins. Yes, God loved you and chose you just as you were, but He didn't plan for you to remain that way. The Holy Spirit, who brought faith into your heart, continues His work in you, changing you to make your heart like Christ's. Through God's amazing transformation process, you are coal-turning-to-diamond!

How does coal become a diamond? Three elements are needed in this transformation, and the first is *time*. A diamond is not formed overnight. It takes a long time for rough, porous, black coal to be completely transformed into a smooth, solid, luminous diamond.

You have probably heard the phrase, "Please be patient; God isn't finished with me yet." It is true! He is continually at work in you, holding you in the palm of His hand, changing and transforming you to fulfill the purposes He has for you, and that takes time—His time. But it is so difficult to be patient, isn't it? The Psalmist reminds you to "be still before the Lord and wait patiently for Him" (Psalm 37:7). Empowered by the

Holy Spirit, you wait patiently, allowing the Lord time to work in you and transform you, trusting that "He . . . will bring it to completion at the day of Jesus Christ." He will continue to work in you until He calls you home to heaven or until He comes again; it is a continual process.

Time is needed to transform that lump of coal into a dazzling diamond. Enabled by the Spirit, you can give the Lord your time. Trust His promise in Matthew 6:33: "But seek first the kingdom of God and His righteousness, and all these things will be added to you." Carve out a regular time to meet with God for *personal devotions*. The Holy Spirit works powerfully through the Word to transform believers in Christ's image. Make time for regular *worship* in God's house. The Spirit continues to fill you as you learn and grow in God's presence, fed by the Word and the Sacraments. Find time for *fellowship*. God uses other Christians in your midst to strengthen and uphold you. Finally, make time for *prayer*. God commands it, and He hears and answers every prayer in His timing and with His wisdom. He grows in you and changes you through prayer; He enables you to let go of your cares and entrust them to Him.

God desires your time! Over time, He continues to transform you, from the inside out, until you sparkle and shine like diamonds. Others can see His reflection in you!

> *Lord, thank You for choosing me and holding me in the palm of Your hand. Continue Your transformation process in me, changing me to have a Christ-like heart. Give me patience as You work in me, changing me over time, that I may be a brilliant reflection of Christ to a world in need of a Savior. In His name. Amen.*

A Diamond in the Making, Part 2: Pressure

> Count it all joy, my brothers, when you meet trials of various kinds, for you know that the testing of your faith produces steadfastness. And let steadfastness have its full effect, that you may be perfect and complete, lacking in nothing. James 1:2–4

Although you began as a dirty chunk of plain old coal, your Father in heaven scooped you up out of the darkness of your sins that filled you and surrounded you. He called you by name and chose you to be His own possession. He cleansed you of your sins and gave you eternal life in Jesus' name. And although God loved you just as you were, He immediately began His work in you, filling you with His Spirit, producing faith in you, continuously working to make a complete transformation, changing you to have a heart like Christ's! Through God's amazing transformation process, you are becoming a diamond, the most precious of all gems!

How does coal become a diamond? Three elements are needed in this transformation, and the second is *pressure*. Constant pressure. A piece of coal deep within the earth feels quite literally the weight of the world upon it. We can compare that to the adversities, pressures, and pain we face in this life. Heavy demands and trials. Pain and sorrow. The effects of the sinful world press in on us from all directions and we wonder "Why?" "Why are You allowing *this*, Lord?" "Why must I endure this?" This burden of a job with too many demands; this heartache over a troubled marriage; this devastation at the loss of a loved one. This battle with depression or illness; this

struggle with a rebellious child; this difficulty with finances—
the list goes on. You have your own list of pressures; no one
escapes them. But God is with us in the midst of them.

Under all this pressure, pain, and adversity, the Lord makes it
possible for you to trust Him, to remain obedient to Him. By
the power of His Spirit, you can trust Him completely for everything and in every circumstance. You may not understand
why you face trials and pressures, but you can cling to the
truth that nothing happens that has not passed through God's
fingers first. He promises to work all things together for your
good (Romans 8:28), even the most difficult and painful trials.

Sometimes the pressures you endure are for the benefit of
someone else; sometimes they make you see your need for the
Lord. Other times you may not see a reason until the heavy,
dark time has passed. Trust Him, that through all life's pressures, He is strengthening you, just as coal is strengthened by
the earth's pressure during its transformation from porous
rock to the hardest mineral on earth. Through times when
your faith is tested most, you can "count it all joy" that the
Lord is using them to develop a full level of faithfulness, commitment, and steadfastness in you, "that you may be perfect
and complete, lacking in nothing." Coal, fully transformed,
and made "perfect and complete," is a diamond. You shine,
reflecting the light of Christ in you!

*Dear Lord, although I may not understand all the
pressures in my life, by Your Spirit, help me to trust You
through them, knowing You use them to make me
steadfast and strong in Christ. May others see
You reflected in me, Jesus. In Your name. Amen.*

A DIAMOND IN THE MAKING, PART 3: HEAT

> Bearing with one another and,
> if one has a complaint against another,
> forgiving each other; as the Lord has forgiven you,
> so you also must forgive. Colossians 3:13

God loves you right where you are. In fact, once upon a time, He chose you and saved you in Christ when you were nothing more than a lump of coal. Your heavenly Father lovingly picked you up off the pile of sin you were in and claimed you as His own possession, sending His Son to die in your place for those sins. From coal, through an amazing transformation to diamonds in the rough, the Holy Spirit is at work in you. And because God has a plan and a purpose for you, He will continually change and transform you more and more into the likeness of Christ, to give you a heart like His.

How does coal become a diamond? Three elements are needed in this amazing transformation process, and the third is *heat*. Intense heat. Deep within the earth, coal is intensely hot, making its way to "diamondhood." Let me ask you: Are there scorched places in your heart where you struggle to forgive someone who has sinned against you? Have you burned with anger over someone else's shortcomings and failures? Have you melted down under the intense heat of hatred, anger, or lack of forgiveness? We struggle with a failure to forgive. We continually fall into the same traps in our complaints against others. Let's face it. In the heat of sin and anger, we need to forgive others, just as we need the forgiveness the Father richly and mercifully gives us. We need to "be kind to one another, tenderhearted, forgiving one another, as God in Christ forgave [us]" (Ephesians 4:32).

As Christian women, we live as saved, forgiven daughters of our heavenly Father. Jesus' blood has cleansed us and set us free from our sins. Not because we deserved it, but because of His mercy. And as a result, we are free to show others the same undeserved grace the Father has shown us, by the power of the Holy Spirit. No healing balm cools and soothes burned, scorched hearts like forgiveness. Just as the intense heat and subsequent cooling of the earth work to change coal to diamonds, so God transforms us through His discipline due to the intense heat of our sin that requires the cooling balm of forgiveness. We undergo further change as we offer others that same forgiveness given to us by our Lord.

Lumps of coal, we were once dirty, black, and porous; under the care of the Creator, who allows just the right amount of heat necessary to produce the desired change in us, we are becoming precious gems. He will keep working in us so our lives shine and sparkle. We are becoming a brilliant reflection of Christ to a dark world in need of the Savior's light of grace.

Father God, I confess my sin of not forgiving others. Help me to forgive, as You have forgiven me for so much more. Continue Your amazing transformation process in me, growing and changing me to have a Christ-like heart, even as You use the intense heat in my life to make that change. May I shine brightly, reflecting Your image to everyone around me. In Jesus' name. Amen.

A GIRL'S BEST FRIEND

[Jesus said,] "I have called you friends. . . . You did
not choose me, but I chose you. . . ." John 15:15–16

"Guess what he gave me for Christmas?" the young woman
cried out in excitement to her friends. "Well, I'll give you a
hint: it's a girl's best friend!" Before she could hold out her
hand to show off the extravagant gift she had received, her
friends encircled her, squealing with delight, jumping up
and down, and shouting, "Let me see! Let me see!" Her hint
had been a dead giveaway: a diamond, of course. A girl's best
friend.

What is it about the diamond that gives it the status of being
called a "best friend"? Let's see . . . It is *costly*—definitely. It is
valuable—no doubt. *Rare*? Perhaps, though diamond mines
produce millions each year. *Beautiful*—of course. It involves
sacrifice: someone has to hand over a lot of loose change in
exchange for one. And it certainly *makes a statement.* But do
these defining qualities of a diamond also meet the criteria for
"friend"?

Can it listen when you talk? Is it there for you when you need
help and reassurance? Suddenly, the "best friend" on your finger or around your neck begins to fall short, doesn't it? These
qualities sound much more suitable to our girlfriends, our true
friends, both *valuable* and *rare*; they walk with us, laugh and
cry with us, and hold us up when we need help. We thank God
for our friends, through whom He often blesses us and takes
care of us.

But even our closest friends cannot compare to the Friend

we have in Jesus. Like our girlfriends, He also listens to us when we talk (only He never puts us on call waiting), and He is always able to be there for us when we need help and reassurance. Can any other friend guarantee that? Even when we are unfaithful friends, He remains true, steadfast, and faithful. Friendship with Jesus is *costly*—for Him, that is. It involved the greatest *sacrifice* of all time: His life in exchange for eternal friendship with us, *making a statement* of unconditional, lavish love and rich grace, saving us from our sins. True *beauty* is found on the cross and at the empty tomb. Only He can walk beside us no matter where we are going or where we have been, offering us perfect words of direction, comfort, and hope. He is our ultimate source of strength.

Is it *rare* to find a friend like this? Jesus is beyond rare; He is one-of-a-kind! Salvation can be found only in Him; it is the most extravagant gift you will ever receive! And get this: He formed your friendship, choosing you and calling you "friend" first. (If Jesus were on Facebook, He would definitely request you to be His friend.) You are unique and *valuable* to Him; He treasures you. By His grace and strength, you not only receive the honor of being called His best friend, but you can be a faithful friend to others, loving them as He first loved you. Jesus is most definitely every girl's best Friend!

Jesus, there is no greater love than the love You have given me, laying down Your life for me. You have called me friend! By Your Spirit, may I be a faithful friend to others, loving them as You first loved me. In Your name I pray. Amen.

A NEW SETTING

And we know that for those who love God all things work together for good, for those who are called according to His purpose. Romans 8:28

Two small marquis-shaped diamonds were set in place on my wedding band by the jeweler, following our request for a custom-designed ring. As the band was united with my engagement ring on our wedding day, the two small stones joined a larger solitaire stone, one on each side of it. They shone brilliantly, as diamonds do, reflecting light while providing a constant reminder of our love for each other.

Unfortunately, the settings were not secure, and nine years later, one of the small stones fell out and disappeared. For several years, we looked down at my lopsided ring wondering what to do with this broken band that held one small marquis on one side and an empty setting on the other. We finally decided to remove the settings, melt down the metal on both sides, and save the small stone for a new setting—a special purpose! While my solitaire stone was once again alone, the little marquis was being prepared for a new setting: a special ring created for our daughter. In its new setting, the small stone has a similar purpose: to shine brilliantly, reflect light, and provide a constant reminder of our love for her.

Are you or a loved one being called according to God's purpose to move from your familiar setting to be placed in a new one? Perhaps the change in setting is unexpected, or perhaps you know it is coming; you know it is needed in order to mend a broken situation. Maybe others have left and your old setting is not the same anymore. Regardless, change is always difficult. The old setting could be your home or community; perhaps it's your workplace or church, or several of these at once. So, maybe you are resisting the change as you look at your lopsided situation and wonder what to do.

Praise God that He sees you in your broken and lopsided situations, and He forgives you in Christ for all of your sins, including your resistance to the change. Through Jesus' death and resurrection, your salvation is secure. His light shines on you and His Spirit fills you, softening your resistance and enabling you to fulfill the purpose He has for you in your new setting: to shine with the same brilliance you had before, reflecting the light of Christ to everyone around you in your new home or community, in your new workplace or church.

God's ways are always perfect. If He has called you to a new setting, it is "according to His purpose." He has a reason and a plan for it, and He will make "all things work together for good." And isn't it exciting to know that you are His *treasured* possession? That He has saved you for a special purpose? He has custom-designed just the right setting where you can shine most effectively and brilliantly reflect the light of Christ to the dark world, so all who see your light shining remember God's love for them in Christ.

Lord, thank You for the settings in which You have placed me, old and new. You work all things together for good, according to Your purpose. Let Your light shine through me in my setting today, that others may see Your love for them in Christ. In His name. Amen.

AFTERGLOW

> When Moses came down from Mount Sinai, with
> the two tablets of the testimony in his hand as
> he came down from the mountain, Moses did not
> know that the skin of his face shone because he
> had been talking with God. Exodus 34:29

A loyal servant of God named Moses faithfully led God's
people, the Israelites, out of four hundred years of slavery in
Egypt by God's miraculous hand. The Israelites found them-
selves in a vast wilderness en route to a land promised to them
by God. In this wilderness, God instructed Moses to climb
Mount Sinai to meet with Him. Moses had the rare privilege of
entering into God's presence on that mountain. To the people
below, God's presence on Mount Sinai looked like a consum-
ing fire. Exodus 34:5 says, "The LORD descended in the cloud
and stood with [Moses] there." It was there on top of that
mountain that the Lord God made a covenant with Moses and
the people. God gave Moses the very words of the Ten Commandments, inscribed on tablets by Moses to bring back down
to the people. Moses stayed with God on the mountain for
forty days and forty nights. When he descended the mountain,
Moses did not realize "that the skin of his face shone because
he had been talking with God." Moses, in the very presence
of God, received the laws of God—words to live by—and left
God's presence changed, radiant, glowing, as his face reflected
the glory of the Lord. Moses had to veil his face because the
people, in their sinfulness, were afraid to stand in the presence
of God's glory.

We have a privilege the Israelites did not have. The promised

Messiah, whom the Israelites had long awaited, has come. Christ, the Messiah, has made a new covenant with us, sealing it with His blood. His death and resurrection paid the full price for our sins. He entered our hearts in the miracle of Baptism. He enters our hearts through the hearing of His Word, and His faith-giving Spirit restores us in His Holy Supper. By faith, we are promised eternal life with Him. We, in the very presence of God, receive the grace of God—faith to live by—and abide in God's Word, in His presence, changed, radiant, glowing! We reflect the glory of the Lord. And because of Christ, we can reflect God's glory with unveiled faces: "And we, who with unveiled faces all reflect the Lord's glory, are being transformed into His likeness with ever-increasing glory, which comes from the Lord, who is the Spirit" (2 Corinthians 3:18 NIV).

Like Moses' face, our faces reflect God's glory. But we have the privilege of remaining in God's presence continually, abiding with Him always because He lives in us and continues to transform us into His likeness, through the power of His Spirit. Does your face radiate Jesus the way Moses' face did in the afterglow of being in the very presence of God? Can those who see your face tell that you are in the presence of the Lord? Do you reflect the image of God in Christ for the world to see? The answer is yes, by the grace of God, who gives you your glow!

Lord, thank You for saving me by grace through faith in Christ Jesus, enabling me to abide in Your presence always! By Your Spirit, enable me to reflect Your glory for the world to see. In Jesus' name I pray. Amen.

BLING!

But you are a chosen race . . . a people for His own possession, that you may proclaim the excellencies of Him who called you out of darkness into His marvelous light. 1 Peter 2:9

Bling is big! It is in the malls and in the magazines; it is on TV and all around your community. Where there are a lot of women, there is sure to be a lot of "bling bling"! Jewelry. Big jewelry. Fun jewelry. Jewelry filled with stones, beads, gems, glitz, and sparkle. Bold, bright, and beautiful necklace and earring sets. Dazzling bracelets and rings. Gone are the days of having just silver or gold in your jewelry box. The trend now is to have bling to accessorize each outfit with the latest colors.

The word *bling* or *bling bling* was added to the Oxford English Dictionary in 2003. It refers to "loud" jewelry (jewelry that really makes a statement), based on the "sound" it makes: "B-L-I-N-G-G-G!" Even our small, simple cross necklaces whisper "bling" as they shine and catch the attention of others because they, too, make a statement.

There is another kind of bling. Do you see it? It's loud and it's bright. It isn't coming from a lamp or through the window. But there is a brilliant glow in your room, and it is coming from—you! Yes, you. No, you don't need to powder your nose; it's not that kind of glow. The glow is coming from *inside* you. You shine brighter than any bauble around your neck. You are priceless; you are valuable beyond compare to the One who gives you your glow. While the world may treasure the bling you wear, God *treasures* you!

Someone cleverly said, "You've gotta use ch-ching to get the bling bling!" In other words, there is cost involved if you want the bling. Guess what? God purchased you at a much greater cost. In His eyes, your value is so great that even in the darkness of your sin He was willing to hand over His Son, Jesus Christ, in exchange for you, choosing you to be His treasure, filling you with the light of forgiveness and faith in Him.

Jesus came into our dark world and flooded it with His marvelous light. Through Christ, God shines the light of His Word into our hearts "to give the light of the knowledge of the glory of God in the face of Jesus Christ" (2 Corinthians 4:6), and we reflect His light beautifully! Bling! Jesus adorns us with His bling as He fills us with His presence, with the gift of the Holy Spirit. While we may put on the bling around our necks, we can't just put on our Jesus bling. We could try to conjure up some fake glow, like that of a sunless tanning spray, but only He who is at work in us gives us the true reflective glow coming from the inside out. Bold, bright, and beautiful, it is a glow that the world cannot help but see. In Christ, we are God's treasured possession, chosen to proclaim the Gospel message, to declare His truth, to sing His praises. As we wear our Jesus bling, we are making a statement to a world surrounded in darkness that the light of Christ reflected in us shines on them! Bling!

Dear Jesus, thank You for calling me out of the darkness of my sin and into Your marvelous light of forgiveness and faith! As Your very own possession, may I declare Your praises, bringing Your light to a dark world, by Your Spirit's power. In Your name. Amen.

BROKEN

He heals the brokenhearted and binds up
their wounds. Psalm 147:3

"Mommy, Mommy! Look!" the little girl sobbed. "It's broken.
Please fix it!" The plastic princess jewelry set had sustained
many hours of hard play, but now the gem-filled necklace had
broken and fallen to the floor, causing several plastic diamonds to fall out of their glue settings and one little princess
to break into tears. Although it would have been easier to buy
another cheap set than to successfully mend this broken piece
of plastic, the mother lovingly took the trinket in her hands.
With a little hot glue and a lot of heavy tape, the necklace was
"as good as new" and a tiara-topped tear-stained little girl
smiled again.

How many broken pieces of real jewelry sit in your case waiting to be repaired? Broken chains, broken pendants, broken
rings. They sit there, unusable and unappealing in their broken
state. Maybe you don't know how to fix them or you are incapable of mending them on your own. Is it time you took them
to someone who can and will?

How many broken pieces of your life are waiting to be repaired
today? Maybe you broke promises you made to others and
have failed to mend them, damaging your relationship as a
result. Is it possible that you have broken the spirit of someone
you love because you continually cut him or her down? Maybe
you come from a broken home or live in one now. Or perhaps
you have broken ties with family members who have hurt you.

Have you suffered a broken heart because someone you love betrayed you or did not return your love?

Although you desperately desire healing, you don't know how to fix what is broken. Because we are sinners, we all live in a constant state of brokenness, unusable and unappealing; we are in desperate need of repair. In our sin, we are completely incapable of mending anything on our own. It is time to take our broken lives to the only One who can. Like the little princess, as adopted daughters of the King, we can cry out, "Abba! Father!" (Romans 8:15). "I am broken, Daddy! Please heal me; bind up my wounds!" Why does God even bother with us in our broken, messed up state? Because we are precious to Him; He *treasures* us! Out of His great mercy and love, He chooses us in the midst of our brokenness and sin, and He nails those sins to the cross of Christ. He lovingly takes us in His hands and heals our broken hearts; He successfully mends our broken lives, binding up our wounds. We are as good as new! By the power of His forgiving Spirit at work in our lives, we can offer the same forgiveness to those who have broken our hearts. We can seek restoration from a broken relationship, and we can ask for forgiveness from those whose spirits we may have broken.

Abba! Father! I am broken. For Jesus' sake, heal me
of my sin and brokenness. Bind up my wounds today.
By Your grace, I am as good as new. In Your Spirit's
strength, enable me to bring the same forgiveness and
healing to others. In Jesus' name I pray. Amen.

CLAY JARS

But we have this treasure in jars of clay, to show
that the surpassing power belongs to God and
not to us. We are afflicted in every way, but not
crushed; . . . persecuted, but not forsaken; struck
down, but not destroyed. 2 Corinthians 4:7–9

Imagine you are unearthing the ruins at an archaeological dig.
The most common items you find are pottery shards—fragments of jars and bowls, everyday vessels used by even the
poorest commoners. Ordinary lumps of clay were formed into
simple containers used to carry water and food. As you continue the excavation, you notice a portion of a vessel sticking
out of the ground and you gently unearth the rest of it, finding
that it is almost entirely intact. It is chipped and cracked, but
almost whole. Gently lifting it to examine it more closely, you
can tell there is something inside. Tipping it over, you gasp as
the ancient clay jar's contents spill out: gold coins and a few
precious gems. Its purpose is revealed; the frail, fractured piece
of everyday pottery contained a family's treasure.

Is there anything more common or plain than an ordinary clay
jar? How could it possibly contain anything extraordinary?
That clay jar is you and it is me. God chooses us to hold the
most precious treasure: the Gospel message—the Good News
of salvation in Christ. But aren't we a rather poor location to
place something so valuable? Frail, damaged jars of clay, we
are not worthy of containing such great treasure.

Despite our unworthiness, our Lord God chose us in the midst
of our sin and redeemed us! He gently picked us up out of

the ruins of our transgressions and saved us, although we are marred and flawed, cracked and broken. Romans 5:8 tells us, "while we were still sinners, Christ died for us." The power of His Holy Spirit works in us through our Baptism and in God's Word to place something extraordinary inside us. We are filled with faith, and we carry the Gospel treasure to the world.

Although there is nothing about us that would attract attention; although we possess no greatness on our own, when the light of Christ shines in our hearts, our purpose is revealed. We possess "the light of the knowledge of the glory of God in the face of Jesus Christ" (2 Corinthians 4:6), and something amazing happens. The power of the Gospel is at work in you and in me, unlikely "containers." While the unbelieving world knows we are frail, weak vessels, it also sees us persist in our Christian walk with a strength that is clearly not our own as we face personal struggles and are afflicted in every way. They hear us speak boldly about Christ, although we are bumped and bruised, persecuted and ridiculed for our words. They watch as we live out our faith even when we are struck down for doing so. We are not crushed; we are not forsaken or destroyed because the surpassing power coming from within us belongs to the Lord! By His grace, others will look right through us and see Christ. We are lowly messengers, fragile and frail, but our task is to carry the treasured Gospel message. The light of Christ shines within us, simple jars of clay.

Dear Lord, thank You for choosing me, a humble clay jar, to carry the priceless treasure of the Gospel. By Your Spirit's power, enable me to share the Good News of Christ to the unbelieving world around me; may Your light shine in me. In Your Son's name I pray. Amen.

DEFINED! PART 1: CUT

> For we are His workmanship, created in Christ
> Jesus for good works, which God prepared before-
> hand, that we should walk in them. Ephesians 2:10

Your Master Craftsman has amazing plans for you. He took hold of you when you were nothing but a chunk of coal, and He chose you as His own, cleansing you and saving you in Christ, transforming you from coal to a diamond in the rough. And He continues His good work in you, refining you and defining you through the power of the Holy Spirit. How does the Master Craftsman—God—define you?

A diamond is described by four qualities: the four Cs of Cut, Color, Carat, and Clarity. It is first described by its *cut*. The master jeweler takes hold of his diamond in the rough. He knows that as he works, each of his diamonds will be unique and special, one of a kind—custom designed. He cuts with precision. Each cut is unique to each stone, made precisely where it will best show the skill of the maker and where it will most effectively reflect light. What cut is best? The master jeweler knows this before he even begins to shape his gems. Will he choose to shape his diamond round, heart, or marquis? Will he shape it into a square, tri-cut, or pear?

Just as every stone is cut and shaped precisely and uniquely by a master jeweler, so your loving Father, your heavenly Master Jeweler, crafts you, defining you by your cut. God knew in advance the good works He had planned for you in Christ Jesus. And because you are His workmanship, He creates in you a unique "shape" with the specific qualities for those precise tasks He has in mind for you. There is no box behind the jeweler's counter containing a backup "you." You have a unique purpose, unlike anyone else's.

"Chink, chink." These are the sounds of the Master's tools. He is developing gifts in you that are uniquely yours. As a master jeweler makes each precise cut in a diamond, envision God doing the same. He shapes you just so—maybe with (chink, chink) an eye for detail, (chink) an ear for listening or for music, (chink, chink) a heart for the disabled, (chink) a mind that loves creativity, (chink) hands for serving meals to shut-ins, (chink, chink) arms that hold little ones tenderly, (chink) strong legs for running the Gospel message to others.

God knows the needs of the people around you, and He designed you specifically to meet some of those needs. Perhaps you don't feel unique or gifted, or you feel that someone else's gifts are better than yours. Don't compare your cut with others. (You can't be pear-shaped if God crafted you to be round!) By the power of His Spirit, you have the ability to be the best you possible, so use the gifts God gave you out of response to the ultimate gift of salvation He freely gives you in Christ.

When you use your unique gifts, you most effectively reflect Christ's light, just as He designed you to do. He shines in you for others to see as you offer up gifts to others that no one else can bring in exactly the same way.

Dear God, thank You for the ultimate gift of salvation that is mine in Christ Jesus. Please continue to work in me through Your Spirit's power; help me to recognize the unique cut and shape You have given me and to use these abilities and gifts to serve others and glorify You. Shine through me, Jesus! In Your name. Amen.

DEFINED! PART 2: COLOR

The true light that gives light to every man was
coming into the world. John 1:9 NIV

The Master Craftsman continues His good work in you, holding you in the palm of His hand. You are His treasured possession, and He is at work, refining you and defining you in His mighty Spirit's power, making you more like Christ. How does the Master—God—define you?

As we are learning, a diamond is described by four qualities: the four Cs of Cut, Color, Carat, and Clarity. The second way a diamond is described is by its *color*. While a diamond may take on a hue or a hint of color, it has very little color of its own. A diamond in its purest form has no color at all. Its job is to reflect light brilliantly. From its many facets, it sends forth various beautiful colors of bright light in many directions. Have you ever held a diamond in the light to test this? It is amazing.

It's interesting, isn't it, that a gem that receives such attention for its brilliance and razzle-dazzle, for its twinkle and its bling, doesn't produce its own light or color. The most precious, valuable, and expensive of all gemstones certainly cannot glow in the dark! All the color, all the bling you see, is a reflection of light coming from above. The master jeweler has made the unique cuts perfectly in each stone to best catch light and reflect it, glorifying its maker. Bling!

If a diamond is kept in the dark, it has no bling, no shine, no razzle-dazzle. We, like the stones, have no light, no sparkle of color, no good coming from within us. Not on our own.

God, in His mercy through Christ Jesus, shines His light in us through the Word and the Sacraments. The Book of John is filled with references to Christ as the light. His light shines into the darkest corners of our sin, filling us with the light of His forgiveness and faith in Him. "In [Jesus] was life, and the life was the light of men. The light shines in the darkness" (John 1:4–5). As He who *is* light shines on us, He fills us with His Holy Spirit, and we become a brilliant reflection of Him. We shine when others see in us the reflection of the love of Christ.

God looks at us on the inside, doesn't He? He does not look at outward appearances (see 1 Samuel 16:7). But humankind does look at outward appearances. That is why God puts the beauty and brilliance of the Lord Jesus within us to be reflected on our faces for the world to see. Because of His reflection, people can pick a Christian woman out of a crowd, not by the beauty of her face but by the beauty of Christ shining through her. Not by the bling accenting her face, but by the bling of Jesus *in* her face.

As a believer in Christ, you wear the color of His reflection. You are defined by this beautiful color and light. His light is evident in you, through the Holy Spirit's power. Others can see a difference. Your expressions and your words, your attitudes, and your actions reveal the light that is in you, and God is glorified! Bling!

Lord Jesus, thank You for shining Your light in me, filling
me with forgiveness, faith, and new life in You!
By Your Spirit, may the color of Your reflection shine
clearly in me. In Your name. Amen.

DEFINED! PART 3: CARAT

Join in imitating me, and keep your eyes on
those who walk according to the example
you have in us. Philippians 3:17

The Master Craftsman continues His expert work in you so
your life shines and sparkles and is a brilliant reflection of
Christ to a world in need of a Savior. The Master takes you,
His diamond in the rough, and lovingly shapes, cuts, and
polishes you, uniquely and beautifully. How does your Master
Craftsman—God—define you?

As we continue to learn, a diamond is described by four qualities: the four Cs of Cut, Color, Carat, and Clarity. The third
way a diamond is described is by its *carat*. The carat describes
a precious stone's size and weight.

You are precious! The Master Jeweler defines you, His precious
stone, by your weight—your influence. You pull quite a bit of
weight. You have a heavy influence on those around you. Do
you realize the impact you have on everyone in your life? Your
attitudes, words, and actions carry a heavy weight, especially
on those closest to you. Do your children or other loved ones
see you spend time in God's Word? Can your family see your
love for the Lord and for others by how you prioritize your
time? Do your co-workers know you are a Christian? Do those
around you in the pews on Sunday morning see a heart of
worship or a distracted heart?

If any of these questions strike a chord and you are feel-
ing convicted right now; if you recognize that the weight of
your words and actions has felt like a heavy burden you have

dropped; if you fear you have failed to walk according to the godly example you have been given—take heart. God's mercy and grace in Christ frees you from the heavy burden of your sin. He lifts the cumbersome weight of guilt and failure off you by forgiving you of all your sins. By His grace, the Lord will use your influence, however imperfect it may be, to accomplish His work and impact lives around you for His good. He continues to pick you up and carry you, forgiving you and redirecting you when your heavy weight of influence has fallen in the wrong direction.

Whose lives do you have the opportunity to influence on a regular basis? Who may have their eyes on you, looking to imitate your example? Pray that the Holy Spirit equips and empowers you to have a heavy impact on them in the weeks ahead. He makes it possible for you to begin a new commitment to read the Bible. He gives you the desire to redirect your priorities so they reflect the importance of the Lord and others in your life. He fills you with a willingness to share your faith at work, to pray for an undivided heart during worship.

Your Spirit-filled enthusiasm, your zeal in your faith, and your love for the Lord are very influential; they bear quite a weight. Those around you will want to imitate you and "walk according to the example" you have shown them, by the grace of God.

Dear Lord, I praise You for Your mercy in Christ. You have lifted the heavy burden of my sin and set me free! Fill me and strengthen me, that my carat—my weight— has a positive impact on everyone in my life so they are drawn to You through me. In Jesus' name. Amen.

DEFINED! PART 4: CLARITY

Do not be conformed to this world, but be transformed by the renewal of your mind. Romans 12:2

The Master Craftsman, who lovingly chose you as His treasured possession, crafts you with a *cut* that is uniquely yours,
with a precise weight—*carat*. Although you already wear the
color of the Master's reflection, He gives you the ability to
shine even brighter, with perfect *clarity*, the fourth quality that
describes a diamond. How does your Master Craftsman—
God—define you?

A jeweler measures clarity by peering into a diamond with a
special instrument to look for inner flaws called *inclusions*. A
diamond is described as having perfect clarity when there are
no inclusions—no flaws—and it is polished to a perfect luster
and flawless shine. We want others to see the love of Christ
shining through us with perfect clarity. Because of His Holy
Spirit, we wear His reflection, so why do we often appear dull
and lackluster? Why does His reflection appear dim? Because
we are so easily dulled and flawed by the effects of our sin and
the world.

Doubt creeps into our minds as we hear so much disbelief
around us. Alternative beliefs, alternative lifestyles, and moral
relativity are subliminally preached to us from every direction
in our world. What is the result? A thin layer of film obscures
the luster of the diamond, or an imperfection or flaw is revealed in it. We fall prey to materialism and greed. Our desire
for the passing treasures of this world becomes greater than
our desire for the eternal treasure of the Lord. Another layer;

another imperfection. We succumb to gossip, lies, and slander. Our tongues are quick to lash out against others. Another flaw. As the influences of this world accumulate, His reflection gets dimmer and dimmer. How can this be? After all, we are Christians; we are diamonds belonging to the Lord! But we are also sinners; we are plain old lumps of coal. We are saint and sinner at the same time; the age-old Christian paradox applies to us today.

This side of heaven, we will not be without flaw; we are sinners, conforming to this world. Yet God sees us with perfect clarity because He looks at us through the lens of Christ. So we are saints in Christ, transformed in Him! How can a diamond's clarity be restored to shine its brightest? When it is daily, continuously cleaned, freshly polished, and healed of its inner flaws. We are cleansed continuously through Christ's saving work on the cross. We come to Him with repentant hearts, and He graciously forgives and renews.

We shine brightest when He is at work in us through His Word. To combat the lies of the world, we must be in God's Word, abiding with Him, and seeking His truth. Healed and transformed by the power of the Holy Spirit, we are able to live out what we are learning in His Word, and thus His reflective glow shines brightest for the world to see. Others may even exclaim, "So this is what the love of Jesus looks like!"

Dear Lord, forgive me for my flaws, as I have sinfully conformed to the ways of the world. By Your grace, cleanse me and transform me, so I may be restored and renewed, so Your light may reflect and shine with perfect clarity in Christ! In His name, Amen.

FOREVER

Give thanks to the LORD, for He is good, for His
steadfast love endures forever. Psalm 136:1

"Forever." A single word was printed next to a larger-than-life
diamond on a billboard, sending a heart-tugging message to
women as they drove by: "If the love of your life gives you a
diamond, he is saying, 'Forever.'" Forever what? Forever he
will love you? Forever he will be committed to you? Forever
he will make payments on the enormous stone he presents to
you, as he promises you "forever"? On a serious note, it is true
that the diamond, more than most earthly gifts, is a beautiful
expression of "forever," since it is the strongest, most durable,
hardest mineral on earth, and it will not wear away or tarnish
or disappear over the course of a lifetime. You will have your
diamond forever, that is, until death parts you.

A diamond promises forever. Where else do we hear this
word? My young child, when he could not imagine having to
grow up some day and leave home, calmed his own fears by
saying, "Mommy, even when I'm big, I will live with you and
Daddy forever!" A young couple, faced with large student
loans and a new mortgage payment, moaned to each other,
"At this rate, we will be in debt forever." A road-weary family
nearing the end of their vacation, still hundreds of miles from
home, complained, "It will be forever before we get home!"

In our finite minds, can we even grasp the full meaning of
forever? We use the term broadly and frequently, even when
we know that the thing we describe does not define forever;
it is not "eternal" or "without end." I am confident that my

child will not live with us all of his life. With diligence and discipline, the young couple will see their debt end, sooner or later. And the vacationing family will eventually pull into the driveway of their home.

Only God can provide us with the fullest and richest meaning of the word *forever*. Our eternal Father was in the beginning, is now, and will be forever; He is without end! In His perfect creation, He made man and woman to live forever in Paradise and in perfect union with Him. But in the midst of that Paradise, the first man and woman were tempted and fell into sin that led to death; it plagued all mankind to follow. "Sin came into the world through one man, and death through sin, and so death spread to all men because all sinned" (Romans 5:12). Sin separated us from our eternal Father, from a life forever with Him. But there is good news! The steadfast, never-ending love of our Creator-God is so great, that He came to us in the midst of our sins with the perfect plan of salvation, promising life forever in one Man, Jesus Christ. "For if, because of one man's trespass, death reigned through that one man, much more will those who receive the abundance of grace and the free gift of righteousness reign in life through the one man Jesus Christ" (Romans 5:17). Death is not the end! When Jesus died in our place, we received eternal life by grace through faith in Him. What ultimate comfort it is when we hear these most reassuring words, "His steadfast love endures forever."

O Lord, thank You for the promise of life forever in heaven, fulfilled for me in Jesus Christ, Your Son. You are good, and Your steadfast love does, indeed, endure forever. In Jesus' name. Amen.

Good Treasure

The good person out of the good treasure of his heart produces good, and the evil person out of his evil treasure produces evil, for out of the abundance of the heart his mouth speaks. Luke 6:45

She wanted to say something nice to her friend. She knew she should, and this was her chance. But he had hurt her feelings so badly, and though he had even sought her forgiveness, she just couldn't let go of his hurtful words: "Maybe if you lost a little weight, someone would actually want to go on a date with you." She kept hearing those words in her head, and they had gotten lodged in her heart, making her bitter. And though she also knew what she ought to say, the words that came out of her mouth expressed the evil treasures of her heart, of her sinful flesh. She sarcastically stated, "Well now, I see *you* haven't been on a date in a while. What happened? Did all the girls gain a little too much weight for your taste?" Ouch. That was mean and nasty, an unnecessary dig in a feeble attempt to get back at him for the hurt he had caused her. Why were her words so evil? She knew she needed to take a look at the condition of her heart. She was in need of a heart transplant.

We all have stories like this, times when our words betrayed the evil condition of our hearts; when the words on our lips reveal the type of "treasures" abundant in our hearts. We want to say something nice, but we allow the hurt and pain of our own sins and the sins of others to fill our hearts. We struggle with an inner battle. We commiserate with the apostle Paul, who laments, "For I know that nothing good dwells in me, that is, in my flesh. For I have the desire to do what is right, but not the ability to carry it out. For I do not do the good I want, but the evil I do not want is what I keep on doing" (Romans 7:18-19). Our sinful flesh wages war within us. But it is no match for the Lord! Again, we can cry out with Paul, "Who will deliver me from this body of death? Thanks be to God through Jesus Christ our Lord!" (Romans 7:24-25). Jesus conquered sin and death on the cross. His all-powerful Spirit is at work in us, defeating the sinful flesh, completely changing the condition of our hearts. The evil treasure of our hearts is removed, replaced by His life-giving Spirit, which produces good treasure; a heart transplant has taken place.

How does He accomplish this heart transplant? The Holy Spirit works powerfully through the Word and the Sacraments, filling us with new life, forgiveness, and faith. God's Word commends us to store up and keep His commands in our hearts (see Psalm 119:11; Proverbs 2:1; 3:1; and 4:21 for a few examples). Hearts filled with God's Word of life will produce good, by the power of His Spirit. Proverbs 4:23 warns us to guard our hearts, because the springs of life flow from them. "For out of the abundance of the heart [the] mouth speaks."

Thanks to the work of the Spirit, we are able to produce good words, not evil; the Lord creates an abundance of good treasures in our hearts! Our words can be used for building up, giving grace to those who hear them (Ephesians 4:29).

Dear Lord, forgive me for the evil words that have come out of my heart. Thank You for the heart transplant You have performed in me, replacing evil with good, by Your Spirit's power! May my mouth speak only good words, giving grace to all who hear. In Jesus' name. Amen.

HIDDEN TREASURES

> If you receive My words and treasure up My commandments with you, making your ear attentive to wisdom and inclining your heart to understanding; yes, if you call out for insight and raise your voice for understanding, if you seek it like silver and search for it as for *hidden treasures*, then you will understand the fear of the LORD and find the knowledge of God. Proverbs 2:1–5 (emphasis added)

The phrase "hidden treasures" brings to mind the image of a chest filled with precious metals and gems that is buried in a remote location. A treasure hunter bears a map where X marks the spot. Searching for and locating the mysterious spot, the hunter digs and finally unearths the old chest, opens it, and stands in awe at the bounty inside.

Perhaps there is an adventure-seeker in all of us. My children and I have read stories of hidden treasures. After reading one such story, my children's eyes glazed over as their imaginations took them to the location where they would find a treasure. As a young girl, I, too, was fascinated with the thought of finding treasure, but I was not sure there was any to be found on our family farm. So I gathered treasures and trinkets, sealed them in a jar, and headed out to the garden to bury my treasure. I even marked the spot. Pleased with my work, I marched back in the house and drew a treasure map. I daydreamed that someone in the distant future would search for my treasure and be thrilled with the find! A few days later, however, impatient with my plan, I dug up my own treasure. Anyone who tried to follow my map would come up empty.

As King Solomon penned the proverb above, he knew of great earthly treasures. While God had blessed him with a wealth of wisdom, He also gave Solomon great riches. Using words inspired by God, Solomon spoke of hidden treasures, knowing it would tickle the ears of his listeners. People of his day also thrilled in searching for hidden treasures and buried riches. These wise words advised them, as they advise us today, to treasure God's Word and His commands, searching for wisdom, insight, and understanding through them. We are to search for these things with the zeal of a treasure hunter. The value of His Word and commandments is far greater than any earthly treasure, for through it we will "understand the fear of the Lord and find the knowledge of God."

Instead of treasuring the things of God, however, we are often caught up in our quest for earthly treasures—the trinkets and trappings of this world—and we often come up empty. We are buried beneath the weight of our sins, unable to dig ourselves out of our hiding spots. But God, out of His rich mercy and grace in Christ, reaches down and lifts us out, saving us from our sins. A cross marks the spot where our Savior laid down His life to save ours. His precious Spirit gives us the desire to seek the Lord with the zeal of a treasure hunter. We follow the treasure map of His Word, which points the way to Christ "in whom are hidden all the treasures of wisdom and knowledge" (Colossians 2:3). As we open God's Word, we stand in awe at the bounty inside; we are thrilled with our find!

Lord, empower me with Your Spirit that I may desire to search Your Word and Your commandments, seeking the greatest treasures of wisdom and knowledge in Christ, my Savior. In His name. Amen.

JEWELRY CLEANER

Wash me thoroughly from my iniquity,
and cleanse me from my sin! Psalm 51:2

My jewelry needs help. And I have a can of foam jewelry cleaner in the hall cupboard that provides just the help it needs. It is wonderful stuff. When I shake the can and press the button, it dispenses cleaner like hair mousse. It looks mild and has no odor; if I didn't know any better, I might place a dollop of it on my dessert. But when I dispense it over my good jewelry, the foam begins to sizzle; it appears to be eating away at my necklaces and rings. Oh, wait! It's just eating away at something *on* my necklaces and rings. As the foam slowly turns into a pool of clear liquid, amazing things begin to appear: bright gold chains emerge where dull, tarnished chains lay just a moment ago. Brilliant, sparkly stones appear where lackluster ones used to be. The film staining all my jewelry is gone in moments.

I know that cleaner can make my jewelry like new again, washing away every external impurity, all the built-up film, and every bit of dirt and grime. So why does my jewelry cleaner sit in the hall cupboard for months or years between cleanings while I walk around with stained, tarnished treasures on my fingers and around my neck?

A man came to Jesus who needed help. He had a condition much worse than the film coating the surface of some jewelry. According to Luke 5, this man was covered with leprosy, a skin disease plaguing his body that was thought to be contagious. He would have been considered unclean by his community, forced to live in isolation from his family. He knew that by approaching others, he risked making them unclean as well. But with great courage and in a beautiful expression of faith, he fell on his face in front of Jesus and begged, "Lord, if You will, You can make me clean" (v. 12). He knew that Jesus could heal him. It is likely that he had heard of the miracles the Teacher was performing; maybe he had even witnessed one. In trust, he asked for cleansing. And Jesus had compassion on him. Stretching out His hand, Jesus touched him and said, "I will; be clean" (v. 13). Instantly, the leprosy was gone!

You and I need help. Our condition is also much worse than a mere stain on the surface. We are full of sin, covered with impurities. Far worse than leprosy, our condition tarnishes and stains us from the inside out. Our hearts are unclean, and so are our lips. We are plagued with guilt; we suffer from a buildup of hurtful things we have said and evil deeds we have done.

We know that Jesus can make us like new by washing us thoroughly from every impurity, from our dirty, grimy sins. So why do we walk around stubbornly stuck in our sins? Jesus provides just the help we need. When He comes to us in the midst of our sins, amazing things happen. Jesus has compassion on us, as He did for the leper. He stretches out His nail-scarred hands and He touches us with His grace. "Be clean," He says to us. And instantly our sin is gone.

Lord, You are wonderful! By Your grace,
You have washed me thoroughly and cleansed me from
my sin, Jesus. Thanks for the forgiveness that is mine in
Your name. You provide all the help I need.
In Your name I pray. Amen.

LIGHT OF THE WORLD

[Jesus said,] "I am the light of the world.
Whoever follows Me will not walk in darkness,
but will have the light of life." John 8:12

It was a mountaintop moment. "[Jesus'] face shone like the sun, and His clothes became white as light"(Matthew 17:2). After a long mountain climb, Jesus, the light of the world, was transfigured on a mountaintop before the eyes of His closest followers, Peter, James, and John. God's glory was revealed in His beloved Son, the One who came to bring light into a dark, sin-filled world; the One whose death and resurrection would lead us out of the darkness and give us the light of life! For a moment, Jesus' disciples actually saw Him in His full radiance and glory on top of the mountain. The heavenly Father's voice spoke from a bright cloud, enveloping them and saying, "This is My beloved Son!" (Matthew 17:5). The glory of our Savior was revealed; the glory of the One who gives us our glow as we follow Him, walking in His light.

Another mountaintop; another climb. This time before the eyes of multitudes of followers, Jesus, the light of the world, gave the Sermon on the Mount, proclaiming a powerful message of light. He told His followers, "You are the light of the world. A city set on a hill cannot be hidden. Nor do people light a lamp and put it under a basket, but on a stand, and it gives light to all in the house. In the same way, let your light shine before others, so that they may see your good works and give glory to your Father who is in heaven" (Matthew 5:14-16).

These words were proclaimed for you, His chosen child, His

forgiven follower. Led by His Spirit, you can reflect the light of Christ into your home, your community, your work—your world. He enables you to be transparent about your faith, to make sure that your light is visible, not hidden "under a basket," but like a "city set on a hill"—on a mountaintop! An unbelieving world learns what Jesus is like by watching you as you walk in His light. And when you falter along the way, God's grace in Christ is there to pick you up and dust you off, giving you another chance to shine.

Even a small light looks bright when everything around it is dark. A huge difference is made when just one person shines Christ's mountaintop light into another person's dark valley. People living in darkness are drawn up to the light, which reveals sins hidden down in the darkness, enabling them to see their need for a Savior and giving them the desire to follow Him too. The darker the environment in the valley of sin, the more attractive, the more valuable, and the more obvious your mountaintop light will be. You reflect His light brilliantly for the world to see, giving glory to your Father in heaven as you shine for Him. One day, all who follow Jesus will see Him in His full radiance and glory, not for a mere mountaintop moment, but for eternity in heaven.

Dear Jesus, You are the light of the world! Thank You for choosing me to follow You, that by Your grace, I no longer walk in darkness but have the light of life. By Your Spirit, lead me to be a light in my world, shining Your mountaintop light before others "that they may see [my] good works" and give You the glory! In Your name. Amen.

MIRROR

Now we see but a poor reflection as in a mirror;
then we shall see face to face. Now I know in part;
then I shall know fully, even as I am fully known.
1 Corinthians 13:12 NIV

I gaze at my reflection in the pedestal mirror that stands in my
bedroom. I think it provides a fairly accurate reflection of me,
although I am not always pleased with what I see. Sometimes
I think it would be more desirable to own one of those fun-
house mirrors (the kind that makes me appear taller and thin-
ner!) instead. My friend's mirror is kind of like that. It is one
of those cheap wall mirrors with plastic backing. The warped
plastic obscures reflections, providing an artificial slimming
appearance. It gives a poor reflection. But even as I stare into
my own mirror, I can alter my reflection merely by tipping the
mirror back at an angle that suits me. Altered or not, the image I see in my mirror is a limited one. I have a limited scope
of the whole "picture" of myself. And there are some parts,
like the back of my head, that I will never be able to see in my
mirror. When others see me face-to-face, they get the whole
picture; they see me fully.

The mirror mentioned by the apostle Paul in the verse above
was likely created from polished metal, which would have provided a blurred, potentially warped image—a poor reflection
at best. This word picture describes you and me as we walk
in faith through this life. God has provided us with a beautiful and accurate reflection of Himself in His Word. Sadly, in
our sinful nature, we warp God's perfect image. We take away
from or add to His Word, obscuring His reflection and tipping

His truth to an angle until it suits our selfish, evil desires. Our finite, imperfect minds can only dimly see or understand His holy and infinite nature, His perfect wisdom and understanding, and His unconditional love for us. That love was clearly reflected on the cross of Christ, where our sins were nailed by a perfect heavenly Father who knows us fully, yet forgives us for Jesus' sake because He *treasures* us! Granting us the gift of salvation by faith, He declares to us in His Word that we shall see Him face-to-face in heaven. When Christ returns, then we will know Him fully, even as we are fully known.

Although we have a limited scope or ability to understand His whole picture, although we know only in part, although we may never fully "see" or comprehend some parts of His perfect plan this side of heaven, by His grace, we possess all that we need for our walk with God through this life. By the power of His Spirit, we possess faith in our Savior through Baptism and God's Word. We can share that faith with others; we can give generously to people as they have need; we can live a life of love as He first loved and treasured us.

As we gaze into our mirrors, we can be reminded that while we are limited by the reflection we see, God sees and knows us fully. By the Spirit's power, may we reflect His perfect image that others would see Him and be drawn to their Savior too.

Dear Lord, thank You for Your perfect reflection that You provide in Your Word. Forgive me for my inability to see You clearly and completely because of my sin. Thank You, Jesus, for Your mercy and salvation, that I will one day see You face-to-face in heaven! In Your name. Amen.

OUR ROCK

The LORD is my rock and my fortress and my
deliverer, my God, my rock, in whom I take
refuge, my shield, and the horn of my salvation,
my stronghold. Psalm 18:2

"Check out the *rock* on her finger! It's huge . . . must have cost a fortune!" A big diamond is often referred to as a *rock*. The word *stone* is also used, though *pebble* sounds too small and insignificant. But *rock*? That's more like it! When called a rock, the diamond sounds impressive, big, strong. And it is. The diamond is the hardest mineral on the earth. Impenetrable and possessing superior strength, another diamond is the only substance that can even scratch it.

While a diamond may be the strongest mineral around, there is a Rock incomparably stronger. Almighty God is praised and glorified for His strength across the Scriptures. More than twenty times in the Book of Psalms, God is called a Rock. King David, the psalmist inspired by God to pen the words above, spoke about what he lived and knew. Running from enemies who threatened to take his life, David often hid in caves and behind large rocks and boulders. Enemy weapons could not penetrate a rock or even come near David when he was safely in such a shelter. God provided these physical strongholds and shelters for David's protection, and it was from these strong-holds that David wrote these words. Similarly, a stone fortress built to surround a city made it virtually impossible for an enemy to attack; inside the high city walls, one was shielded and safe. David knew of that kind of stronghold too.

More impressive than the largest caves and strongholds, bigger than boulders and rocks, higher than the tallest fortress, was God's all-powerful protection over David. Knowing his true refuge came from Him, David reverently praised the Lord for His almighty protection, strength, and deliverance. God was his Rock! What more appropriate word could be used to describe an all-powerful God who was mighty to save him and capable of providing King David with complete protection?

The same Lord shields you and me, providing ultimate physical and spiritual protection. God is our Rock! Although our own sinful flesh taunts us and we pridefully try to protect ourselves, it is to no avail. Although our enemies threaten us, preying on our weaknesses, although the evil one aims his weapons of deception at us, attempting to make us fall for his lies, we can take refuge in our Rock: the Rock of Jesus Christ, God's own Son, our Fortress and our Deliverer. Our Rock delivers us from our sins and fills us with the Spirit's strength, providing protection for our every need. Our Rock overcomes our enemies, making us strong in our Savior. Our Rock shields us from the devil and his weapons, combating and crushing his lies with the truth. He alone possesses superior strength. Incomparably impressive!

The next time you see a large, impressive diamond—a real rock—praise God for His mighty deliverance and strength in Christ, and proclaim with David, "The Lord is my rock!"

Dear Jesus, You are my Rock! I praise You for Your deliverance and protection. Fill me with Your Spirit that I may take refuge in You, sure of my salvation in my Savior. In Your name. Amen.

PIRATES

[Jesus said,] "The thief comes only to steal and kill
and destroy. I came that they may have life and
have it abundantly." John 10:10

"Show me the way to your treasure!" the pirate captain
sneered as he and his band of buccaneers jumped aboard the
royal ship, which carried the king's wealth. The terrified crew
members were forced to point the way to the ship's storehouse
of gold and precious gems, the costly cargo they were carrying.
Seizing not only the treasure but also the ship, the wicked and
ruthless pirates threw the king's crew overboard without a moment's hesitation, in a merciless display of evil.

Steal and kill and destroy; that is what pirates do. They are
filthy thieves, robbers of the sea. These treasure-hungry
scoundrels will stop at nothing to seize the booty they seek.
Recently, I was reminded of their nasty ploys as our family
viewed an old film filled with pirates and ships and based on
a classic theme of good versus evil. Although the pirates were
cunning and crafty, they could not outwit the good captain
and his crew. Following a fierce final battle, the crew prevailed;
they defeated the evil pirates once and for all.

Sadly, we often romanticize the pirate's image on film and in
books. Many a child has dressed up as a pirate, innocently
dreaming of high-sea adventures and treasure chests filled
with riches and jewels. But real pirates were and are an enemy
and a threat to every honest ship that has sailed.

We must beware of a much more menacing pirate—the thiev-
ing enemy, Satan, who tries to jump aboard into our lives and

seize us, the King's precious cargo. The enemy is cunning and crafty, so we must always be on the alert. Scripture tells us that our adversary "prowls around like a roaring lion, seeking someone to devour" (1 Peter 5:8). Maybe his methods are more subtle than the average pirate, but he is more ruthless and merciless. He captures our attention, entices us with the treasures of this world, and tries to force our eyes off the Lord. He points the way of worldly pleasures and personal gain. He preys on our weaknesses, and we fall into the temptations and sins that easily ensnare us. Satan sneers as he thinks he has us in his grip, fooling us with his evil ploys.

In His almighty power, God, "the King of all the earth" (Psalm 47:7), provided a Savior for us, removing us from the grip that sin, death, and the devil once had on us. In Christ's cross, our King prevails, defeating the enemy once and for all and throwing the filthy thief overboard; the final battle has been won! Out of the riches of His mercy, Jesus shows us the way to life everlasting; in fact, He came that we may "have life and have it abundantly"! Through the power of His Spirit at work in us, we can resist the devil and he will flee from us (see James 4:7). Our Savior has laid up for us a storehouse of riches in heaven, our greatest treasure.

> *Dear God, King of all the earth, You have won the final victory in Christ! I need not fear the enemy; You defeated him at the cross, winning for me new life in Your name. Fill me with Your Spirit, that daily I may resist sin and the devil, keeping my eyes fixed on You and the promise of eternal life, my greatest treasure! In Jesus' name. Amen.*

PRECIOUS IN HIS SIGHT

May my life be precious in the sight of the LORD,
and may He deliver me out of all tribulation.
1 Samuel 26:24

"Jesus loves the little children, all the children of the world,"
our Sunday School sang off-key and with all our might. "They
are precious in His sight!" we shouted. Looking at my little
sister, I knew it was true; she was precious in His sight. She
was a rare jewel! For a few brief years, she was able to belt out
those words with the rest of us; that is, when she stood still
long enough. Lisa was "hyperactive" as defined by the doctors
in her preschool years. They would later learn that Lisa was
having small seizures that affected her behavior. Over the next
several years, the seizure activity worsened, damaging more
and more of her brain. Although my parents sought all the
medical care available, there was no cure for the rare degen-
erative disorder that plagued Lisa's body.

Over the years, I often cried out to God in anguish for my little
sister: "If Lisa is precious in Your sight, why would You allow
something so awful to happen to her?" Even as I cried out, I
received the Savior's peace and strength. I know that my family
did too. God gave us the ability to trust Him despite the dif-
ficulties Lisa's disease placed on us and the pain it caused her.
We trusted that He was holding His precious gem, my sister, in
the palm of His hand.

Today, Lisa lives in a home for adults with severe mental
disabilities. She receives excellent care and a lot of love from
caretakers and family. Although I may not understand why she

has had to endure so many trials, I know that my sister's life is precious in the sight of the Lord. She is a chosen and baptized child of God, treasured and forgiven; her salvation is certain. In her limited capacities, she is a joyful person with a ready smile and a quick hug. Although she does not speak or sing anymore, she touches many people with her life. I trust that God is using Lisa's precious life to show them His grace and that He is glorified through her. One day, she will be delivered out of all the tribulation she has endured in this life. One day, she will see her Savior face-to-face and sing with the angels around God's throne!

Our lives are precious in the Savior's sight. We may cry out to God in anguish because we do not understand why He has allowed something awful to happen to us or to someone we love. There will be trouble, pain, and hurt in all our lives as a result of the sin in this world. But we have Good News! Jesus said, "In the world you will have tribulation. But take heart; I have overcome the world" (John 16:33). He overcame sin and death when He died for us. We are chosen and forgiven in Christ; our salvation is secure. We are His treasured jewels—His precious gems. The Lord gives us His peace and strength, enabling us to trust Him in the midst of trials and tribulation. One day, we will all be delivered out of our tribulations. We, too, will see our Savior face-to-face and belt out our praises with the angels around the throne of God!

Lord God, I praise You for choosing me and that my life is precious in Your sight. In the strength of Your Spirit, enable me to trust You through every tribulation. Use my life to show others Your grace. Be glorified through me today! In Jesus' name. Amen.

PRICE TAGS

For I am the LORD your God, the Holy One of Israel,
your Savior. . . . You are precious in My eyes, and
honored, and I love you. Isaiah 43:3–4

"Check out the price tag on that little gem!" "Ooh, that must
be really nice—just look at its price tag!" "Compare these price
tags and notice the difference in quality!"

We place value on most material possessions based on their
price, by the little tag hanging from them at the time of their
purchase. Like the pair of exquisite diamond earrings for
which we saved our money—they are far more precious to us
than the cheap imitation bling we purchased for a few dollars.
The designer dress in the department store, priced way beyond
our budget, impresses us much more than the knockoff at a
discount store, sold for a fraction of the price. The more expensive car gives a smoother ride and includes more amenities
than the economy model. Even if we boast about a bargain we
have acquired, we love to share the original price too, because
the perceived value of that item is increased when we do.

We can't always afford the high-dollar options in our lives, can
we? (Like the real diamonds, the designer dress, or the classy
car.) The financial sacrifice is just too great.

It is one thing to place value on items, based on their price.
But how do we value people? Do we subconsciously put a
price tag on them? Do we look down on someone because she
cannot afford a nice car or name-brand clothing? "Hmm, she's
not worth much." Do we eye another woman quite differently
when she has a high social status? "Wow, she must be worth

a lot." Do we look with a critical eye at the size of a woman's diamond and value her by the "price tag" on her hand?

You are precious in God's eyes. He highly values you, but not with the value the world gives; He doesn't price you based on what you have or have not done; He doesn't label you with worth because of your financial portfolio. But if there *were* a little price tag hanging from your ear, it would say something like this: "Not for Sale." You are too highly treasured; you already belong to the Lord. Or maybe it would say, "Sold to the Highest Bidder: God!" "You were bought with a price" (1 Corinthians 7:23). The Lord your God loves you so much that He paid the ultimate price for you. He purchased you with His own Son's blood, making the greatest sacrifice of all time. Jesus' death and resurrection saved you from sin, death, and the power of the devil, forgiving you for the price tags you have judgmentally placed on others. Through the power of the Holy Spirit, you are filled with the Savior's love and given the ability to see others as He sees you: God's precious possession, honored, loved, and worth far more than all the bling that money can buy.

Lord, forgive me for putting price tags on people, judging them with worldly value. Thank You for sacrificing Your own Son to purchase me. In Your power, help me to see others through Your eyes, as precious, honored, and loved. In Jesus' name. Amen.

PRICELESS

> [Jesus said,] "The kingdom of heaven is like a merchant in search of fine pearls, who, on finding one pearl of great value, went and sold all that he had and bought it." Matthew 13:45–46

Popsicle sticks and hot glue, pipe cleaners and modeling clay. These were the primary supplies used by our three children to make countless treasures and gifts for my husband and me several years ago. When Mother's Day or Father's Day or our birthdays (or any day deemed special by our kids) arrived, we could count on receiving a one-of-a-kind homemade gifts from them. Sometimes our treasure was wrapped; other times it was hidden behind their backs and then revealed with a dramatic "Ta-da! Here it is!" They showered us with creations uniquely their own: a Popsicle raft with miniature clay people onboard; a replica of our kitchen with a tiny model of me inside it; a set of three crosses reverently created with Jesus on the middle cross. His final words, "It is finished," were neatly attached in a tiny bubble caption. And there were many more gifts like these, each a special treasure.

Perhaps these treasured gifts would have little or no significance to someone else, but they were so important to us, we could not even place a value on them that was high enough to cover their sentimental worth. The word that best describes them is *priceless*. Our children poured time, creativity, and love into their works of art that graced our dresser tops for years. And we wouldn't give up our gifts for all the treasure in the world. They are, indeed, priceless!

As special as these treasures are, they certainly cannot compare with the greatest treasure by far: the kingdom of heaven. Jesus' parable of the pearl of great value illustrates for us just how priceless it is. Like the merchant who willingly gives up everything he has so he can buy the fine pearl he has found, we should daily be willing to give up all that we have to follow Jesus. "To seek first His kingdom and His righteousness" (Matthew 6:33). To "count everything as loss because of the surpassing worth of knowing Christ" (Philippians 3:8).

Are we willing? In our sin, we act as though the things of this world possess a greater value than the priceless gift of salvation in Jesus Christ. We prize the passing things of this world more than the eternal gift of God; we cling to the earthly things more than the heavenly ones.

Unlike the merchant who searched for his pearl, God doesn't have to search to find us. We are His unique creation. He knows right where we are, stuck in our sin, and yet He chooses us anyway. We are *treasured* and priceless! We are of such great value to Him that He gave up everything to save us, claiming us as His own. He bought us at the ultimate price with His Son's precious blood. Christ proclaimed, "It is finished!" Salvation is ours. His Spirit moves in us and makes us willing to follow Him. By His power, we can proclaim, "There is no greater gift than knowing Jesus and having salvation in His name!"

Lord Jesus, You have given me Your priceless kingdom through faith. Move me by Your Spirit that I would be willing to give up everything to follow You. Help me to treasure Your priceless gift of salvation above all else. In Your name. Amen.

SOLITAIRE

It is the LORD who goes before you. He will be with
you; He will not leave you or forsake you. Do not
fear or be dismayed. Deuteronomy 31:8

All alone, she sank into her chair, staring at the empty living
room furniture around her. She remembered a time when it
used to be full. In her mind she could still hear the laughter
of her children from many years ago as they would chase one
another around the room, then plop down together for the
family's favorite TV show. As her mind fast-forwarded a few
years, she could hear the squeak of the front door, followed
by the familiar words, "Mom, we're home," as her teens ran in
the room and "crashed" onto the furniture, recalling for her
the adventures of their day. Fast-forwarding again, she could
hear her husband's soothing voice coming from the chair
next to hers: "I know it is difficult for you with the kids grown
and gone, but now we have the chance to enjoy each other's
company!"

Now his chair sat empty too. And she was alone—a solitaire
like the diamond on her hand. She smiled through tears as
she looked at her wedding ring. Her husband had chosen the
solitaire diamond—a single stone—insisting on it because it
reminded him of their union: formerly two, they had become
one. As she twisted the ring on her finger, she thought about
the new meaning *solitaire* had in her life now. A widow whose
children lived across the country, she was utterly and completely alone.

Feelings of dismay and despair crept over her. How could she possibly face another day as a solitaire? Then her eyes fell on a familiar sight: her husband's Bible still lay on the end table between their chairs. "Thank You, God!" she cried out. In her pain and loneliness, she had forgotten. A sob caught in her throat as she recalled the truth she knew—the truth that her late husband had shared with her often, especially during his final days. The truth that *God was with her*. That she was forgiven in Christ and saved by grace through faith! By the power of His Holy Spirit, she could cling to the promise from His Word that He would never leave her. Though people in her life might leave—even die—she would never be alone. She need not fear or be dismayed. She could face each day knowing God had gone before her, preparing her way, and that He also walked beside her as each day came.

Overwhelmed by our pain and loneliness, we, too, may despair, thinking we are all alone. But God's Word tells us otherwise. Our heavenly Father loves us with an everlasting love; we are tenderly *treasured* by our Lord, who showed us the fullest extent of His love when He gave us His Son, Jesus Christ. Jesus suffered a greater degree of pain and loneliness than we will ever know when He went to the cross alone, taking on our sins and the sins of the whole world, dying for us so we would never have to face a day as a solitaire. Our Lord Jesus walks with us, filling our loneliness and healing our pain as only He can.

O Lord, I praise You that You are with me always!
By the power of Your Spirit, help me trust that You walk
beside me, Jesus. You will not leave me or forsake me.
In Your name. Amen.

THE BRIDE

I delight greatly in the Lord; my soul rejoices in
my God. For He has clothed me with garments of
salvation and arrayed me in a robe of righteousness, as a bridegroom adorns his head like a priest,
and as a bride adorns herself with her jewels.
Isaiah 61:10 NIV

A bride-to-be dreams of her wedding day, when she will be
united in holy matrimony with the man she loves. She dreams
about the ceremony and the celebration of their love that
will be shared with family and friends. She dreams about the
details and the decorations, the colors and the music. And perhaps most of all, she dreams about what she will wear. Will her
white gown be floaty chiffon or shiny satin? Will she wear a
string of pearls or sparkling diamonds? Will she choose a thin
veil to drape over her face, or a dainty wreath to encircle the
crown of her head? She is delighted as she dresses on her wedding day, covered in a dazzling white wedding dress, adorned
with beautiful jewels and other accents.

As a bride delights in her elaborate covering for one special
occasion, how much more should we delight in our Lord every
day? As she rejoices in her new husband, the bridegroom, so
we ought to rejoice in God our Savior, for He has covered our
sins in Christ Jesus, clothed us with garments of salvation, fit-
ted us with dazzling white robes of righteousness.

In our sin, we are unclean. As Isaiah 64:6 says, "All our righteous acts are like filthy rags" (NIV). We possess no ability
to be made right with God on our own. "None is righteous,

no, not one" (Romans 3:10). He picked us up out of the dirty filth of our sin and cleaned us off, fully forgiving us through Jesus' death and resurrection on the cross. The shedding of His blood completely covered all our sins. We are wrapped in forgiveness; we are made righteous in Christ through faith! As Romans 3:22 reminds us, "The righteousness of God [comes] through faith in Jesus Christ for all who believe." Our salvation is assured.

Just as a bride glows, dressed in her beautiful jewels, how lovely are we, dressed in His garments of salvation, in His exquisite robes of righteousness! So great is the Lord's love for us, He rejoices over us "as the bridegroom rejoices over the bride" (Isaiah 62:5). In fact, we, the Church, are called the Bride of Christ. Ephesians 5:25–27 tells husbands to love their wives just as Christ loved the Church. In Revelation 19:7–8, there is great rejoicing in heaven as the multitudes give God glory, "for the wedding of the Lamb [Christ] has come, and His bride [the Church] has made herself ready. Fine linen, bright and clean, was given her to wear" (NIV). The Bride is cleansed and robed in Christ's righteousness, ready to be presented to Him.

Overflowing with the love of Christ and filled with His Spirit, we can't help but rejoice in Him who rejoiced in us first, who chose us as His Bride! We are delighted, and the world can see our glow. As we clothe ourselves with Christ (Romans 13:14), may we sparkle and shine, showing the world our Savior, that they may be clothed in Him too.

I praise You, Lord, that You have arrayed me in Your robe of righteousness, covering my sins completely! Strengthen me by Your Spirit to clothe myself with Christ, that the world may see You shining in me. In His name. Amen.

THE MISSING STONE

Rejoice with me, for I have found the coin
that I had lost. Luke 15:9

My mother-in-law wears a unique "mother's ring" with a
custom-designed setting that contains six colored gemstones,
the birthstones of her six children. The ring is a special gift;
each stone in the ring is precious because it represents that
child. One day many years ago, our nephew Ethan was sitting
on Grandma's lap, asking about her ring. She patiently ex-
plained, "This ring reminds me of all of my children. The first
stone—your uncle Preston; the next—your aunt Patti, and the
third stone—your mom . . ." After she pointed to all six stones
and named all six children, Ethan gave her a very concerned
look. "But, Grandma, you're missing a stone! Where is Aunt
Debbie's stone?" Ethan was certain that I must be one of
Grandma's children too. I married into his family when he was
only a year old. As one of the family, he thought I, too, should
have a stone in her ring. Thankfully, all the stones were intact.
None were missing. But what if one *had* fallen out? My mother-in-law would have combed the house, swept the floors, and
looked intently to try to find it. Not only is there real value in
each stone, but more important, the sentimental value in my
mother-in-law's stone-filled ring makes it priceless. Though
the other five stones would be in place, if one were lost, she
would *rejoice* upon finding it!

Jesus tells a parable of a woman who has lost one of her ten
silver coins. The silver coins He mentions are drachmas, and
each is about a day's wages. It is not a large sum of

money, but valuable to the woman. Although she has nine other coins like it, the lost coin is so precious to her that she lights a lamp, sweeps her house, and seeks diligently until she finds it. When she does, the woman is ecstatic. What do you think she does once she finds her one-day's-wage coin? She celebrates! She calls her neighbors and her friends to join her for a party. And she rejoices!

Jesus' words that follow are priceless, as He explains the meaning of the parable: "Just so, I tell you, there is joy before the angels of God over one sinner who repents" (Luke 15:10). All of heaven rejoices with God when one of His precious children who once was lost is now found. If a woman would comb her house to search for a missing stone, or another woman would light a lamp to hunt for a missing coin, how much more will our heavenly Father, who delights in us and *treasures* us, move heaven and earth to seek and find one child who is lost? Our Lord went to the greatest lengths to save us when we were lost, unrepentant sinners: He sent His Son to the cross to die in our place, sacrificing His life to redeem ours, giving us the extraordinary gift of salvation and faith in His name. Adopted into His family through Christ, we are His own precious children! (There is a stone in His ring for each of us!) He rejoices over us, priceless pieces of the family of God.

Heavenly Father, thank You for sending Your Son to the cross to save this lost sinner. Fill me with Your Spirit and give me a continually repentant heart, that I may honor You. In Your Son's name. Amen.

THE REAL THING

[Jesus said,] "I am the way, and the truth,
and the life. No one comes to the Father except
through Me." John 14:6

My older sister had a piece of jewelry that fascinated me. I loved to look inside the blue velvet box that held the most incredible diamond ring I had ever seen. The enormous solitaire stone sat high and proud on its band. Occasionally, I would slip it onto my finger, hold it close to my face, and gaze in the mirror, pretending I was a rich and famous movie star with a fortune in jewels. Why wasn't my sister showing off her treasure? Later, I learned the truth: it was an imitation diamond; a $10 substitute for the real thing. No wonder she didn't display this giant gaudy bling on her hand.

An artificial diamond made merely of cheap cut glass is certainly no substitute for the real thing. At first glance, we are easily deceived. But if we know anything about diamonds, we will quickly see the differences. Cut glass contains countless flaws in clarity; a pure diamond contains none. When examined closely, the artificial stone reveals porous, weak glass that wears down quickly, eventually exposing its false identity. A true diamond is the strongest substance on earth, able to withstand years of wear without damage or change.

Are you or someone you know being fooled into believing a cleverly cut artificial diamond is authentic? It may be packaged to look like the real thing. Be cautious of claims; test your diamond to see if it is real. If a diamond can be harmed or scratched by any other substance, it is a cheap imitation.

Just as an imitation diamond looks real enough at first glance, alternate religions may also have initial appeal. They make alluring claims. We must be cautious of these claims, testing them against the Scriptures. (If we don't know what God's Word says, we may fall for anything.) While accepting cheap, imitation diamonds may only cause hurt feelings, dabbling in alternate religions causes much deeper damage. All other religions contain countless flaws; when examined closely, they reveal their greatest flaw: man-made rules that rely on our works for salvation. Their false identity is exposed. The one true Christian faith is centered on God's grace in Christ, revealed in His pure and perfect Word. Nothing in this world is more powerful! Through the centuries and countless attacks against it, His Word remains unharmed and unchanged.

The Bible tells us that Jesus is the only way to salvation. He saved us not by works, but by grace through faith alone (see Ephesians 2:4–9). Other world religions are not alternate roads to heaven, to salvation, to eternity with God. Praise God for His free gift of forgiveness and faith in Christ, the only way to heaven. Filled with His presence, we are true gems—real *treasure*. People are attracted to the one true faith when they see the light of Christ shining in us. With the help of the Holy Spirit, they see in us the "real thing."

Dear Lord, forgive me when I have fallen for the imitation claims of others instead of listening to Your truth. Continually fill me with Your Spirit and point me to Your Word, so that others would be attracted to Christ shining through me. In Jesus' name I pray. Amen.

TREASURES FOR THE KING

And going into the house they saw the child with
Mary His mother, and they fell down and
worshiped Him. Then, opening their treasures,
they offered Him gifts, gold and frankincense
and myrrh. Matthew 2:11

They had traveled far, perhaps for months, to find Him. A careful study of a star, which announced for them the birth of the "King of the Jews," had prompted foreigners to travel in search of this King. These Wise Men followed the star that led their way, until they found what they sought: the Christ Child. And when they arrived at the house in Bethlehem, what joy must have filled their hearts as their eyes beheld the King, the little boy Jesus. They fell down, bowing low before Him, and they worshiped the Christ Child, giving tribute to the King of the Jews. They brought with them treasures for the King and presented to Him the finest of gifts: gold, frankincense, and myrrh. Costly and precious, these were gifts fit for a king.

Centuries earlier, the Israelites brought gifts to their Savior-God, King over all the earth, who had chosen them as His treasured possession. In tribute and worship, the people brought gifts before the altar of the Lord. By God's commands, they offered sacrifices and gifts for the atonement of their sins. The first and the best of all the fruits of their labor were dedicated and given to their God, their Provider and Redeemer.

We are God's chosen people in Christ, His *treasured* possession. He has delivered us from a fate far worse than human slavery. We were slaves to sin and could not free ourselves from the grip of sin, death, and condemnation. God, in His mercy, gave us the greatest gifts ever: the forgiveness of sins, life eternal, and salvation in Christ. His sacrifice provided final and complete atonement for our sins and the sins of the whole world. Filled with His life-giving Spirit, we rejoice in our Provider and Redeemer, the giver of all good and perfect gifts (James 1:17). He gives us the desire and the ability to honor and give tribute to Him.

But what gifts can we possibly bring to the Savior, who has given us all that we have? As we worship Him, we are bringing treasures for the King. "By the mercies of God, [we] present [our] bodies as a living sacrifice, holy and acceptable to God, which is [our] spiritual worship" (Romans 12:1). By His grace, we dedicate our lives to the Lord, desiring to serve Him obediently in whatever He calls us to do. We give our firstfruits—our tithes and offerings—for the work of His Church. By the power of the Holy Spirit, we bring all these treasures and gifts before His altar of grace; these are gifts fit for the King.

One day, all nations on earth will acknowledge Jesus as the King of kings and the Lord of lords. They, too, will come and worship Him. "At the name of Jesus every knee should bow . . . and every tongue confess that Jesus Christ is Lord" (Philippians 2:10-11). What joy will fill our hearts as we behold our King face-to-face one day, in our promised land of heaven.

Dear God, thank You for Your gift of eternal life in Christ Jesus! Give me the desire to serve You obediently, to dedicate my life to You, to continually offer these treasures for You, my King. In Jesus' name. Amen.

Make the most of your devotional journey with the *Treasured Retreat Kit*

Packaged on an easy-to-use CD-ROM, this kit has everything you need for a successful women's retreat: leader's presentation with PowerPoint slides, participant handouts, planning guide, decorating ideas, timeline, and promotional tools.

Your retreat can't get any easier ... just add women!

If you like this devotional, you might also like *Beautiful Feet*, a pocket-sized book featuring 30 devotions based on Romans 10:15: "How beautiful are the feet of those who bring good news!"

To order call 1-800-325-3040 or visit www.cph.org